Sophie's Kittens

by Leonie Bennett

Editorial consultant: Mitch Cronick

CONTENTS

Words in **bold** are explained in the glossary.

My cat Sophie

Sophie is a silver **tabby** cat.

She is two years old.

Sophie has a fat tummy.

Going to the vet

The **vet** checks that
Sophie is not ill.

He feels Sophie's tummy.

Sophie is going to
have kittens.

Vet

7

Sophie's special place

Sophie looks for somewhere to have her kittens.

The garden is too cold.

The kitchen is too noisy.

This big box is just right.

It is warm. It is quiet.

Wow – my cat's a mummy!

Sophie has four kittens.

The kittens drink **milk** from Sophie.

Then they go to sleep.

Look at the new kittens

The kittens are three days old.

They can't see.
They can't walk.

The kittens sleep a lot.

They sleep together to keep warm.

Watching the kittens grow

Now the kittens are two weeks old.

They can see.

They can walk.

Soon they use the **litter tray**.

Sophie licks the kittens to keep them clean.

Growing up

Now the kittens are four weeks old.

They can eat **solid food**.

This kitten is
the biggest.

He eats a lot.

Tail

The kittens like to play with
Sophie's tail.

Busy kittens

Now the kittens are ten weeks old.

They run about, play and fight.

They like to bite.

They like to lick.

Look out! Kittens like to scratch.

19

Saying goodbye

Two of the kittens are going
to new homes.

I say goodbye to them.

Now Sophie has just
two kittens.

Soon they will go to live in new homes.

But I will keep Sophie.

Glossary

litter tray
A tray full of little stones that cats and kittens use as a toilet.

milk
The drink produced by a mother to feed her kittens.

solid food
Proper food made from meat or fish.

tabby

A cat with dark markings on a lighter coat.

vet

An animal doctor.

Index

Copyright © ticktock Entertainment Ltd 2008
First published in Great Britain in 2008 by ticktock Media Ltd.,
Unit 2, Orchard Business Centre, North Farm Road, Tunbridge Wells, Kent TN2 3XF
ISBN 978 1 84696 759 7 pbk
Printed in China

We would like to thank: Penny Worms, Shirley Bickler, Suzanne Baker and the National Literacy Trust.

Picture credits (t=top, b=bottom, c=centre, l-left, r=right, OFC= outside front cover)
Marilyn Storey at Skidoosh British Shorthaired Cats: OFC, 1, 2, 5, 6, 8t, 9, 10-11, 12, 13, 14, 15, 16, 17, 18, 19, 21.
Superstock: 4, 8b, 20.